CANDIDATES, CAMPAIGNS & ELECTIONS

DO

CANDIDATES, CAMPAIGNS & ELECTIONS

Projects ★ Activities ★ Literature Links

by Linda Scher and Mary Oates Johnson

SCHOLASTIC
PROFESSIONAL BOOKS

New York ● Toronto ● London ● Auckland ● Sydney
Mexico City ● New Delhi ● Hong Kong

Cover design by Vincent Ceci and Jaime Lucero
Interior designed by Drew Hires
Illustrations by Drew Hires

Cover photograph: Wayne Estrup/The Stock Market

Poster concept: Karen Baicker
Poster design: Solutions by Design

ISBN 0-439-16055-3
Copyright © 2000 by Linda Scher and Mary Oates Johnson. All rights reserved.
Printed in the U.S.A.

12 11 10 9 8 7 5 4 3 2 1   6 7 8/9

Dedication

For John Bremer—teacher, mentor, and dear friend

Acknowledgments

Special thanks to the Board of Elections of
Wake County, North Carolina.

TABLE OF CONTENTS

INTRODUCTION

Advertisers, disc jockeys, and sports announcers know that Americans love contests! Once every four years, our nation engages in the most important, hard-fought, hotly debated contest that a democracy ever holds—the presidential election. Yet only about half of the eligible voters actually take part in the contest by casting their vote for one of the candidates. And voter turnout is even lower during off-year elections when only local, state, and Congressional representatives are running for office.

Through the activities in *Candidates, Campaigns, and Elections*, you can help your students become active in the American political process. *Candidates, Campaigns, and Elections* offers ideas to get students thinking, writing, and speaking about elections. They will learn that elections are more than annoying sound bites and commercials on television. Elections are about real candidates and about issues of importance. Elections are also about the process of campaigning itself, about using the media, and building support. By studying this process and engaging in it themselves, students will become more educated, informed citizens, able to play a part in our democratic system.

Candidates, Campaigns, and Elections contains activities, games, information, handouts, and literature tie-ins for students of different ability levels and different learning styles. Students will learn the chronology of an election, the tricks to writing a good campaign speech, the method of analyzing a speech for propaganda. They will follow a candidate throughout an election and report on his or her campaign and participate in a mock election.

Using the Poster

The poster bound in the back of the book explains the presidential election process. If you are teaching an election unit during a Presidential Election season, be sure to refer to the poster as you and your students discuss the various points along the road to inauguration. You may want to add stick-on notes at certain points to indicate the outcomes of primaries, vice-presidential candidate selections, and the winners of the actual election.

Candidates, Campaigns, and Elections is a flexible resource. You can pick and choose from the information and activities presented in this book that you feel are the most appropriate for your class. Enjoy!

ELECTION BASICS

What makes our country work? In our over 200-year-old democracy our success as a nation has much to do with our politics—the process of selecting leaders. While in some countries today, the changing of leaders still takes place with street fighting and machine guns, this process has been a peaceful one in the United States since George Washington first took office. From the town meetings of New England to the mayoral and council meetings that heat up boroughs, parishes, and counties across America, we choose our leaders by voting and we do it in a sometimes heated but almost always peaceful and orderly way.

Americans choose their leaders in an exciting, multistep process. Each step along the way, especially on the road to the White House, has its own special vocabulary. This section offers activities for understanding government and the election process and its basic vocabulary.

Getting Started

Your students probably know more about voting and elections than they think. Many may have voted in class, at camp, or in clubs. Some students may even have won elections—for student council, club offices, or camp monitors. Discuss ways students make "democratic" decisions at home (on movies and other recreational activities, where to eat or what to eat, what to watch on television or which radio station to listen to in the car, curfew or house rules); at school (student government, classroom activities); after-school clubs or sports, social or religious organizations. Although many of the activities students name may not involve formal elections, they require many of the same decision-making skills students will use when they become voters.

Also encourage students to tell what they know about local, state, and federal government elections.

KWL Chart

Conclude your discussion by making a KWL (What We Know, What We Want to Learn, What We Learned) chart or bulletin board about elections like the one shown here. Have students list what they already know about elections in the first column. Write the questions that arise from your discussion in the middle column. Refer to the chart, adding and answering questions, as the class learns more about elections. Be sure to review the chart as you finish your election unit.

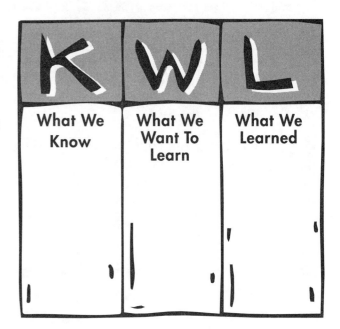

"Jigsawing" to Build Background

In order for students to get everything they can from the activities in this book—and eventually become knowledgeable participants in our democratic system—they should have some prior knowledge about our government. This "jigsawing" technique will help your students create some helpful common prior knowledge, and it will also put greater responsibility for learning on the students themselves.

Divide the class into five groups of about equal size and label the groups A, B, C, D, and E. Tell students these groups are their "home" groups. Within each home group, each member should be assigned a number. For example, if there are 25 students in your class, divide the class into 5 groups, and each group will have members 1, 2, 3, 4, and 5. Explain to students that they will work in different groups to become experts on one kind of government, such as local or state, or one branch of the federal government (executive, judicial, and legislative). Have all the students who have been assigned the number 1, work on becoming experts on local government; have all those assigned number 2 become experts on state government; and so on, until all students are working in an expert group. Explain that after they've become experts, they will return to their home groups and share what they've learned.

Give each expert group a copy of the *Government Fact Sheet* Activity Page (see page 23). Have the students use books;

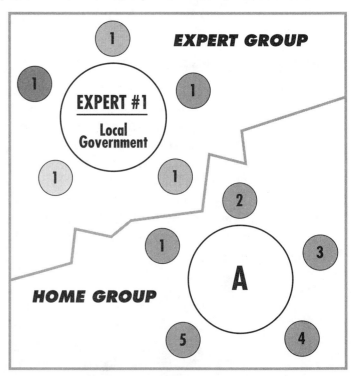

magazines; the Internet, if available; and newspapers to gather as much information as they can to answer the questions on the task sheet. (See Resources on page 80.) They can also call local government offices to find the answers to questions. Students should be prepared to share what they have learned with their groups both orally and visually using charts or posters they have prepared.

Literature Link

The Voice of the People: American Democracy in Action
by Betsy Maestro and Giulio Maestro
Lothrop, Lee, and Shepard Books, 1996

About the Book

Reading this book is a great springboard for introducing students to our government and the election process. Beginning with Election Day, the Maestros explain the basic features of the American democratic system. They present the types of government, the federal system, the balance of powers, and elections. The last five pages of the book contain interesting facts and additional information. Giulio Maestro's watercolor and pen and ink illustrations add to the warm, inviting feel of the book.

As you Read

Each page of *The Voice of the People* contains at least one complete paragraph and the discussion of one topic. Suggest that students create a summary book. Assign pages of the book to one or more students depending on the size of your class. Have them write one sentence summarizing the information on each page you are assigned. Combine all the pages to have a complete summary. Make a cover for the summary book out of construction paper and staple the book together.

A group of students might also enjoy presenting a skit about one topic from *The Voice of the People*. Good topics for skits include election day, how a democracy works, how a democracy is different from a dictatorship, or the powers of the three branches of government.

After You Read

Help your students to gain a deeper understanding of our democratic system by comparing it to other governments throughout the world. Have each student choose a different country to research. You might have them work in groups depending on the kind of governments they are researching, such as dictatorships, monarchies, and so on. Encourage them to use graphic organizers such as Venn diagrams to compare our government to the other country's.

Vocabulary Builders

While learning about elections students will encounter many unfamiliar terms. You can pick and choose from the strategies that follow to help your students learn electoral process vocabulary.

Words in the News

Have students make a list of all terms that they associate with the election process. (See the Glossary on page 77 for additional terms.) Make a master list of terms on the chalkboard. Write each term students have chosen on a large sheet of poster paper. Have students bring in newspaper and newsmagazine articles using these terms and post them on the board under the appropriate heading. Before posting their articles, students should underline key terms and summarize their articles for the class. Encourage students to use context clues to discover the meaning of the terms. Provide students with copies of the Glossary so students can check that they understand what the terms mean.

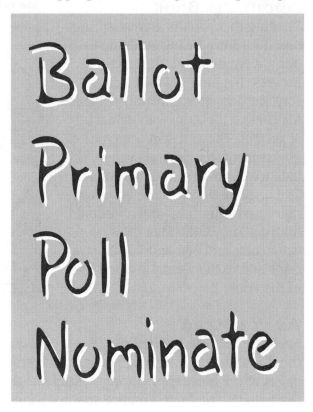

Then have students, working in pairs, choose five words. Ask them to write a paragraph using all five terms correctly. Have students copy their paragraphs over, leaving spaces for their five key terms blank. Have them list these words at the bottom of the page. Pairs can exchange lists, complete the paragraph, and return the paragraph for checking to the original pair.

Political Jeopardy

Invite students to play a game of "Political Jeopardy" using the vocabulary terms they pick up during their election study. To play the game, divide students into small groups. Have each group make up a series of answers to questions that use students' vocabulary terms. For example, Answer: Democratic Party; Question: What is a political party? Answer: Democratic Candidate for President; Question: What is Al Gore?; Answer: Philadelphia; Question: Where was the Republican National Convention held? Since some answers may fit more than one question, the teacher can be the final judge of correct answers.

Electionary

Play a game of Electionary using the playing cards on Activity Pages 24-25. Students can cut out the cards, color the backs, and then fold and tape the cards. You may want to laminate them before they are used. This game uses four players and all cards are dealt. Play goes in a circle with the first player pointing to a card in the hand of the person to his or her right. The player holding the card reads aloud the definition of the term on the card. If the player who has pointed to the card correctly names the term, he or she receives the card, which is placed to the side in the player's winner's circle. If the player does not name the term correctly, he or she does not get the card. Play then continues with the next player pointing to a card in the hand of the person to his or her right. Play goes clockwise around the circle. When a player has no cards, he or she is out of the game. The person with the most cards after four rounds of play wins. The game is most fun if a timer is set before play begins and each round of play is completed within a specified time.

Polling Place: place set aside for voting

Registration: signing up to vote by filling in your name and other information about yourself on a special form

An Overview of the Electoral Process

A "Work in Progress"

If you are teaching an election unit during a presidential election year, this activity can become a "work in progress." Have students begin a mural or collage for the classroom illustrating each of the stages in the electoral process. Have students use original drawings as well as pictures from magazines, newspaper headlines, campaign banners, and bumper stickers to make their mural. Working in groups, students can illustrate a different section of the mural: 1) Candidates announce 2) Candidates campaign in Republican and Democratic primaries 3) Major parties hold conventions and third party activities, if any 4) Party nominees for President on the campaign trail 5) Election Day 6) And the winner is 7)Inauguration. Since some parts of the mural can be completed before others, this can be a work in progress with some groups planning their parts of the mural while others have already completed theirs. By inauguration time, your work in progress will be a classroom masterpiece.

It's Primary

Every race begins with the candidate's announcement that he or she is planning to run for office. In the race for President, candidates usually make their announcement at least one year and sometimes two years before Election Day. The primary elections are the races that narrow the field. In these elections voters decide who their party's candidates will be. Many states have primaries in which all eligible voters can participate. Candidates who hope to win the race for President must enter primaries to win their party's nomination. Most presidential primaries take place between January and June of a presidential election year. Some of the earliest contests are in Iowa, New Hampshire, and Louisiana. Super Tuesday in March has become a day when many states mostly in the South hold primaries. A big win in an early primary can help a candidate in raising funds and gaining the support of other elected officials in their political party.

In the 2000 presidential election, there is no incumbent, or person running for office who already holds the office of President. This makes it more likely that candidates from both parties will have members of their own party challenging them for the nomination. In many elections there is an incumbent trying for a second term as President. This candidate does not usually have any members of his own party running against him for the nomination. Usually there are two sets of primaries—one for Democrats and one for Republicans. A voter can cast a ballot in one primary or the other, but not in both. In primary elections candidates from the same party also compete for the chance to run for the Senate and the House of Representatives as well as for state and local offices.

Instead of primaries, a few states have caucuses attended by members of a political party. At this meeting, members select delegates to state or national nominating conventions. Sometimes the first round of caucuses takes place throughout the state in many different communities. At these meetings delegates also choose candidates to run for state and local elections.

At the Races

Some weeks before primary season begins, on a large, heavy sheet of oak tag, create a long circular race track to be placed on the bulletin board. Mark the track off into 20 segments of roughly the same size. Clearly mark the starting and finish line. Divide students into groups representing each of the candidates competing for President in the Republican and/or Democratic presidential primaries. Have each group cre-

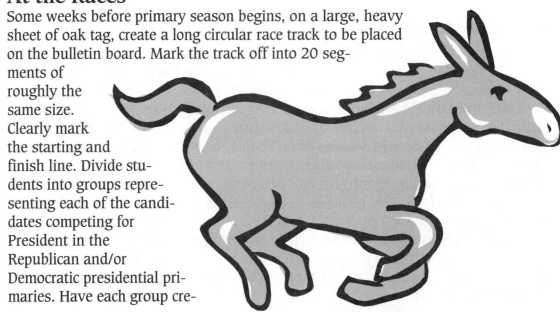

ate a paper symbol to represent their candidate. Instead of making symbols, students may decide to glue newspaper or magazine faces of their candidates to the figures on the *At the Races* Activity Page 26. Each group will be responsible for tracking its candidate's standing in the primary, using newspaper and television reports. This activity works best if students follow at least 10 primaries over the course of the primary season. As candidates drop out, the date of their departure from the race should be noted on the track. Groups can advance their candidates along the track in the following order:

1. Candidate wins 60 percent or more of vote = 2 segments
2. Candidate wins 40 to 60 percent of vote = 1 segment
3. Candidate wins 20 to 40 percent of vote = 1/2 segment
4. Candidate wins less than 20 percent of vote = no movement

As students track their candidates around the track, they will find that a few never leave the starting gate, while others are stalled midway. Only a few get close to the finish line and only one wins the race.

For the File

Every four years on Election Day voters vote for a President and a Vice President. But they also may be voting for members of the House of Representatives, the Senate, governor, and for local leaders. (See page 12 for an activity that will help students gain an understanding of how local, state, and federal governments work.) Distribute the *Sample Ballot* on page 27. Have students pick out an example of a national race, a state race, and a local race shown on the ballot. Explain to students how ballots are marked in your community. In most places voters use punch cards, optical scanning devices, or mechanical or electronic voting machines with levers. In a few places, particularly rural areas in the Midwest, paper ballots are still used.

DID YOU KNOW?

In many major American cities, the mayor is elected by less than 10 percent of those eligible to vote.

Working in small groups, have students use the fact sheet on Activity Page 28 to begin compiling information on candidates running for national, state, and local offices in their community. Among the offices students might choose from are the following:

National: President, Vice President, Senator, Representatives
State: Governor, Lieutenant Governor, State Legislators
Local: Mayor, City Council, Sheriff, County Commissioners, School Board

If students can find a picture of each candidate in the newspaper, a newsmagazine, or in the candidate's campaign literature, this information can also be added. In the space marked "What We Know about the Candidate," the group might put information about the candidate's qualifications for office, a quote from the candidate explaining why he or she is running or expressing views on a particular issue. Collect the fact sheets in a special "For Your Information" or FYI file. Set aside a special corner of the room for your FYI file. Put each fact sheet in a separate folder and add additional news clippings on the candidates as the campaign season progresses. After the election, have the students who prepared each fact sheet, record the outcome of the election on the fact sheet.

A good place to get a complete listing of local and state races is the county Election Board, the municipal or township clerk, clerk of court or the voter registrar. Depending on the state, telephone numbers for these people can be found in the telephone book under such listings as Elections or Voter Registration. Another source for this information is the Federal Election Commission. Their address is: Federal Election Commission, 999 E Street, NW, Washington, DC 20463. Their telephone number is 1-800-424-9530.

Electoral College
In the United States, the President is voted for twice. The first election takes place in November on Election Day when registered voters go to the polls to cast their vote for the person they want for President. This vote is called the popular vote. A second election occurs about one month after Election Day in December when a group of about 538 people called electors representing the members of Congress from the fifty states plus three electors from the District of Columbia meet. This group is called the Electoral College. It is their vote, not the popular vote, that determines who will be President.

Here's how it works. On Election Day Americans are actually deciding how the electors will vote one month later. Explain that each state gets a different number of electors. This number is based on a state's population. After each ten-year census, the exact number of votes given to each state may be adjusted somewhat depending on whether the state has lost or gained population. Each state gets a number of electors equal to its two senators plus the number of representatives it has in the House of Representatives at the time of the election. For example, in 1996, California had 2 senators plus 52 members in the House of Representatives for a total of 54 electoral votes. States with more people get more electoral votes than states with smaller populations.

In each state, the candidate who wins the election for President gets all the electoral votes of that state even if the race is very close. For example, in 1996, Bill Clinton won a close race against Bob Dole in Arizona, beating Dole by a little more than 31,000 votes. Yet Clinton received all 8 of Arizona's electoral votes. The official winner of the United States election for President is the candidate with the largest number of electoral votes.

The electors for each state meet in their state capitals on the first Monday after the second Wednesday in December. The electors cast their ballots which are sealed and sent to the president of the United States Senate. The electoral votes are counted in a joint session of Congress held usually on January 6.

The Top Ten

For this activity, the class will need the map of the United States showing how many electoral votes each state has which is found on Activity Page 75. Have students study the map and name the states that they think are likely to be most important to each candidate's strategy for winning the election. Have them find the top ten states with the most electoral votes. Ask students to think about some ways the candidates might show that these state are important to their campaigns. (Students may suggest frequent visits to the states, large campaign organizations in the state, spending more money on campaign advertisements and mailings in the state.)

Winner Takes All

Use this activity to help students see the difference between the popular and the electoral vote. As a class pick a Candidate A and a Candidate B for president. These candidates do not have to be living people. For example, they could be Lincoln and Jefferson or they could be non-politicians—musicians, actors, scientists, athletes. Try to pick two candidates who are somewhat equally popular with students so that the vote is not a landslide in either direction. Have students cast ballots in a one-person, one-vote election. This will be the class's popular vote. After ballots have been cast and collected, divide the class randomly into six groups representing six different states: California (54), Idaho (4), New York (33), Rhode Island (4), Texas (32), Montana (3). Make sure that there are an odd number of people in each group so that there are no ties in the voting. Assign each group the same number of electoral votes as the state it represents has in the 2000 election. Within their groups, have students vote a second time for the same candidates. Students should vote as they did in the popular election. Emphasize that this is a "winner-take-all" arrangement with all the votes of the group going to the candidate with the majority vote. Tally the electoral votes from each group. Compare the results of the popular election and the electoral votes and discuss how it is possible for the two methods of election to produce different results.

Registration and Voting

Many students and adults have no idea how citizens register to vote. Most are surprised at how easy and simple the process is. Explain to students that there are three requirements for voting in the United States. Voters must be at least 18 years old, citizens of the United States, and residents of the town or city in which they want to vote. People who have been convicted of a serious crime lose their right to vote.

Much like getting a library card, new voters must register, or fill out a special registration form. On the form new voters write their name, address, and date of birth and also must show some proof their age, usually a birth certificate. The exact place of registration varies from state to state. New voters can register at the town hall or city hall. New voters can also register by mail with registration forms available at public libraries or they can register when getting or renewing a driver's license. Registration prevents election fraud. By registering every voter, officials make sure that no person votes more than once during an election. On Election Day, each voter's name is checked off a list of registered voters in a particular area.

A Registration Simulation

To simulate the registration process, select five students to serve as members of the class Board of Elections. Board members conduct a voter registration drive. In the election simulation on page 60, this same group can also locate polling places, prepare ballots, and oversee the mock election. At this time, however, their main roles will be to write a description of voter qualifications for students who would like to register. Qualifications might be as follows: Voters must be citizens of the United States, at the school for at least thirty days, and over a certain age depending on the age of students in the class. Have students present their requirements, discuss them, and post the registration requirements in the classroom. Give the Election

Board the *Voter Registration Form* on Activity Page 29. Have the Election Board members duplicate enough copies of the form so that everyone in the class can have one, but do not give out the forms.

Set aside a corner of the classroom with a table for registration and a specified time such as fifteen minutes each day for registration. Have Election Board members set up a schedule for sitting at the registration table and registering classmates using the Voter Registration Form. For added impact, registrars can have students repeat aloud a Voter Declaration:

> I am a U.S. citizen. I have lived in ____(city) and _____(state) for 30 days before the election. I will be at least____years old by Election Day. I am not registered to vote anywhere else. If I have been convicted of a major crime, I have my rights as a citizen back.

If students are planning to have an election simulation (see page 60), you may specify that registration will close at least one week before the election so that registration forms can be checked. Explain that no one who is not registered will be able to vote.

When the registration period is completed, have the Election Board alphabetize the forms and make a master list on legal-size paper of all registered voters.

Get Out the Vote Posters

Explain to students that in recent decades the number of voters, particularly in the age group 18 to 24 has been dropping. There are many reasons for low voter turnout, but many non-voters don't believe their one vote will make a difference. As a class, have students discuss the following question: If it was your job to get new, young voters to register to vote, how would you do it? Have students brainstorm suggestions. Then working in groups, have students make posters

that encourage young people to register or explain how registration is done. Others might create special Get Out the Vote posters targeted to elderly voters, parents of young children, or people who have just become citizens. Posters could also have a theme such as Why Vote?, It's Your Right, or Voting Is Easy. Give an award for the five best posters and display them in halls or the cafeteria.

Some students may be interested in finding out more about organizations working to get out the youth vote. One such group is:

> Rock the Vote
> 10950 Washington Blvd, Suite 240
> Culver City, CA 90232
> Telephone 310-237-2000

You can find them on the Internet at www.rockthevote.org. This group makes commercials for youth-oriented television and radio stations like MTV. Their get-out-the vote public service ads feature well-known musicians like Madonna, Pearl Jam, and Hootie and the Blowfish, urging young people to participate in elections.

Students can also discuss ways they can take action in an election even before they reach voting age. Among the activities they might identify are reminding adults to register and vote, becoming active in student council, passing out literature for a candidate, and keeping track of current elections. In many states elementary and middle school students are able to participate in mock elections that closely simulate actual presidential elections through an organization called Kids Voting. To find out if Kids Voting has a program in your community, you can contact

DID YOU KNOW?

In the 1988 election for President only 29 percent of citizens between the ages of 18 and 24 voted. This compared with 50 percent for the total voting-age population. In 1996, voter turnout among young voters was a little better. Over 32 percent of eligible voters ages 18 to 24 voted; this compares to 49 percent for all ages in 1996.

> Kids Voting USA
> 398 South Mill Avenue, Suite 304
> Tempe, AZ 85281
> 602-921-3727

You can find them on the Internet at www.kidsvotingusa.org.

Name _____

Government Fact Sheet

I am gathering information about _____.

[kind or branch of government]

Describe the officials who make up this kind or branch of government.

_____
_____
_____
_____
_____

How are the members elected or appointed?

_____
_____

How long are the terms of office?

_____
_____

Where do they work?

_____
_____
_____

What are their responsibilities?

_____
_____
_____
_____
_____

Electionary
GAME CARDS #1

Cut out cards on the black lines, then fold on the dashed line.

Polling Place:
place set aside
for voting

Election Day :
the first Tuesday after
the first Monday in
November

Registration:
signing up to vote by
filling in your name
and other information
about yourself on a
special form

Political Party:
an organization of
people who share simi-
lar ideas about how to
govern the nation and
work together to gain
power by electing its
member to public office

Primary:
an election between
members of the same
party who seek to be
selected as their
party's candidate

Delegate:
a person who is
chosen to act for
others at a meeting

Candidate:
a person who runs
for political office

National Convention:
a meeting of members
of a political party
held every four years
(usually during July or
August) to nominate a
candidate to run for
President

Electionary
GAME CARDS #2

Cut out cards on the black lines, then fold on the dashed line.

Electoral Votes:
the votes cast by members of the Electoral College. To win a presidential election, a candidate must win a majority of these votes.

Nominate:
to propose a candidate for political office

Inauguration:
the ceremony which includes the taking of an oath that takes place at the beginning of a President's term of office

Opinion Poll:
a survey of people to find out what they think

Incumbent:
a person already holding a political office

Sound Bite:
a fragment of television videotape, usually nine or ten seconds in length

Landslide:
an overwhelming political victory

Third Party:
a party organized as an alternative to the two major parties

At the Races

Use newspapers or magazines to find pictures of the candidates.
Then tape them on the correct party symbol.

REPUBLICAN

Picture of
Candidate

DEMOCRAT

Picture of
Candidate

Name _____

Sample Ballot

OFFICIAL BALLOT FOR THE GENERAL ELECTION
November 5, 1996

To vote, complete the arrow ◄━ ━◄ at the right of all candidates of your choice,

including write-ins, like this ◄━━━ ━◄

Read all instructions carefully before voting!!

For President and Vice President of the United States
You must vote separately for President and Vice President
You may vote for ONE party.

Democratic	◄━	━◄
Bill Clinton		
Al Gore		
Republican	◄━	━◄
Bob Dole		
Jack Kemp		
Libertarian	◄━	━◄
Harry Browne		
Jo Jorgensen		
Unaffiliated	◄━	━◄
Ross Perot		
James Campbell		

Please Note
The above candidates are excluded from the straight party ticket.
They must be voted upon separately.

For straight party ticket
(You may vote for ONE party)

Democratic	◄━	━◄
Republican	◄━	━◄
Libertarian	◄━	━◄

For United States Senator

Harvey B. Gantt	Dem	◄━	━◄
Jesse Helms	Rep	◄━	━◄

Ray Ubinger	Lib	◄━	━◄

For Member of Congress 4th Congressional District

David E. Price	Dem	◄━	━◄
Fred Heineman	Rep	◄━	━◄
David Allen Walkter	Lib	◄━	━◄

For Governor

James B. (Jim) Hunt, Jr.	Dem	◄━	━◄
Robin Hayes	Rep	◄━	━◄
Scott D. Yost	Lib	◄━	━◄

For Lieutenant Governor
(You may vote for one)

Dennis A. Wicker	Dem	◄━	━◄
Steve Arnold	Rep	◄━	━◄

For State Auditor

Ralph Campbell	Dem	◄━	━◄
Jack Daly	Rep	◄━	━◄
Robert J. Dorsey	Lib	◄━	━◄

For State Attorney General

Mike Easley	Dem	◄━	━◄
Robert H. Edmunds	Rep	◄━	━◄

Name _____

An Election Fact Sheet

Office _____

Name of Candidate _____

Political Party _____

What We Know about the Candidate

_____

_____

_____

_____

_____

_____

_____

_____

_____

_____

Outcome _____ Date _____

Prepared by _____

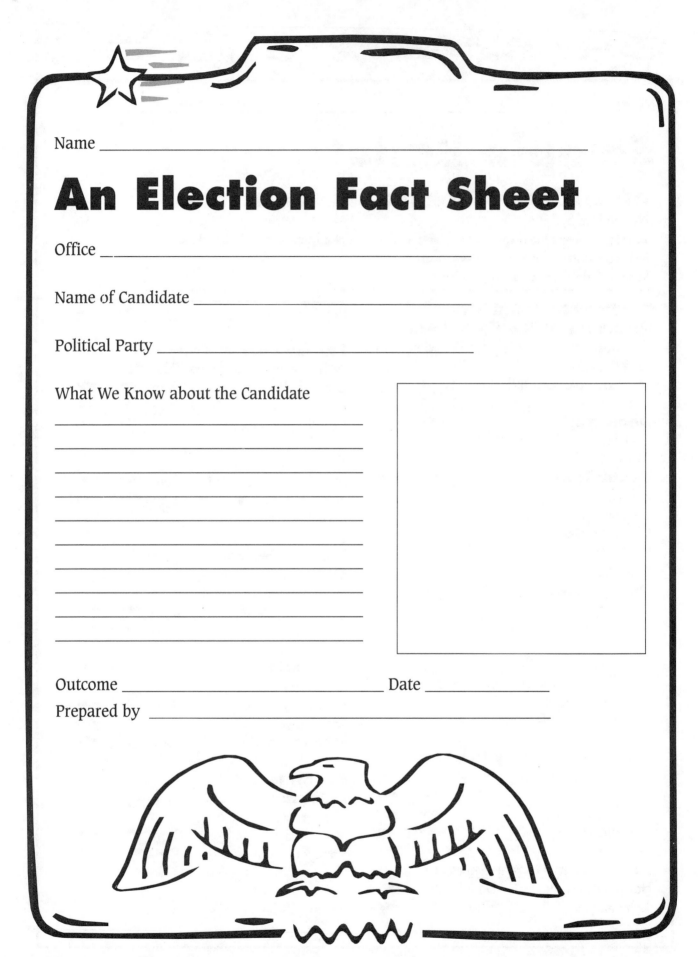

Voter Registration Form

Last Name_____

First Name_____

Address
(Number and Street) _____

_____

_____

City_____County_____

State_____

Date of Birth_____

Place of Birth_____

Signature_____

Date_____

Witness_____

Date_____

City or town where registration
was held _____

WARNING! If you sign this card and know it to be false, you can be convicted of a crime and jailed for up to five years, or fined, or both.

USING NEWSPAPERS AND TELEVISION TO TEACH ABOUT ELECTIONS

During an election campaign, voters are bombarded with information about candidates. Some of this information is objective—such as newspaper reports and analysis, television newscasts, and panel discussions by political reporters. But much of the information comes from the candidates themselves or from their supporters and is often biased. In television and radio commercials, campaign literature, and speeches, candidates try to put themselves in the best possible light. Candidates want to get elected and their campaign materials are intended to convince readers and viewers to vote for them—and not for their opponent. Looking carefully and critically at the media is an important skill that students can use throughout their lives. The activities that follow encourage students to analyze the media and to draw their own conclusions about the completeness and accuracy of election coverage.

Analyzing Newspaper Coverage of Elections

Begin this section by inviting students to suggest the many different sources from which voters learn about candidates: newspapers, radio and television newscasts and advertisements, debates, direct mail campaign literature, public meetings. List responses on the board. Discuss with students the kinds of information each source provides.

- *Which sources are likely to be most slanted or biased in favor of the candidate?*
- *Which sources are most likely to give an objective or unbiased picture of the candidate?*

Election News Scavenger Hunt

This activity will serve to familiarize students with the election information presented in a newspaper. You will need to collect newspapers published during a primary season or an election campaign in order for this activity to work. You might also ask each student to bring in a newspaper on a day when there is likely to be election news, such as the morning after a heated primary, a presidential debate, or a visit by candidates to the local area.

Before beginning, have students identify the various sections of the paper. Ask students which sections are most likely to contain campaign and election news (national and local news sections, editorial pages). Then divide students into pairs or small groups. Supply each group with a newspaper and Activity Page 42, *Election News Scavenger Hunt*. Give students fifteen or twenty minutes to complete their search. If students cannot find one of the scavenger items in their own newspaper, you might have them trade newspapers with another group after a certain period of time.

Classes can also be divided into groups with local newspapers, groups with newspapers from the state capital or a different part of the state, and groups with national newspapers such as *USA Today*. Each group can make up its own Election News Scavenger Hunt, using the newspaper it has been given to form a list of election-related information. Have groups exchange newspapers and complete the scavenger hunt created by the other group. After the scavenger hunt is over, the class can compare and contrast the different types of information found in the different newspapers.

As a variation on this activity, some groups might be given newsmagazines such as *Time* or *Newsweek* instead of newspapers. Students can compare the types of election information each offers.

Election Scrapbook

For this project, each student chooses a political candidate and creates a scrapbook about him or her. The cover can be made from a collage of campaign photos, brochures, and even bumper stickers of the candidate. Students should collect newspaper articles about the candidate and paste them on the interior pages. Students might also want to include quotations from the candidate, pictures of the candidate with the student's own captions, a short biography of the candidate listing his or her experience and qualifications, and a page describing the office for which the candidate is running. If students can find any political cartoons about the candidate, these can be included as well.

Analyzing an Election News Article

Have students bring to class news articles about candidates and election campaigns. Have students write a short summary of their articles and answer through discussion or in writing the following questions about their article:

❥ *Does the headline seem for or against the candidate or neutral?*
❥ *What can you learn about the candidate's stands on issues from this article?*
❥ *What can you learn about the candidate's qualifications for office?*

❧ *Are there any words or phrases in the article that suggest how the reporter feels about this event or about the candidate?*

❧ *Does the reporter use any words or phrases that influence your opinion or impression of the candidate?*

❧ *What impression of the candidate do you get from reading this article?*

❧ *What were some questions about the candidate that this article did not answer?*

❧ *Would this article help you decide whether or not to vote for this candidate? Why or why not?*

Comparing Headlines

In the summer of 1999 when George W. Bush was competing with John McCain, Steve Forbes, and other candidates for the Republican nomination, newspapers reported the results of a poll of New Hampshire voters which asked what Republican they favored for President. George W. Bush was already a strong favorite of many Republican voters. In this poll as well he was the favorite, getting the nod from 40 percent of those polled. John McCain was a distant second as the choice of 16 percent of voters. Headlines in three different newspaper results reported the same results as "Bush Slipping with New Hampshire Voters," "Bush Holds onto Strong Lead," and "McCain Edges Closer to Bush."

Write these headlines on the board. Discuss the impression each gives the poll results.

❧ *Which headline puts a positive "spin" on the election results for Bush? for McCain?*

Headline Collage

Divide students into groups. Assign each group a political candidate running in a current race. Candidates can be competing in national, state, or local elections, but should be candidates likely to be mentioned in local or state newspapers. Over a two-week period, have each group cut out or write down any headlines they see about the candidate they have been assigned. If students have been assigned an incumbent, remind them that they can also look for articles about this official doing his or her job. At the end of the collection period, each group can make a drawing or collage of their headlines. Group members can pick out headlines that help or flatter the candidate and shade them one color and shade negative headlines with a different color. Students might also want to include a photograph of their candidate in the collage. The finished collages can be displayed on a bulletin board under the title "Election Headliners."

Write Your Own Headline

Look for articles about the outcome of an election, a candidate taking a stand or voting on an issue, or a campaign event attended by a candidate. Remove the headlines from the article. Give students copies of the same article. Have each student write a headline for the article. Compare headlines and notice how differences in wording influence impressions of the news report.

33

Help Wanted: Outstanding Leaders Needed

Examine the classified section of the newspaper with students. Have students find examples of different kinds of job ads that list the education or skills required for the job. As a class, discuss the personality traits, skills, education, and experiences that might help a person become an exceptional President, senator, governor, or mayor. Then have each student pick an elective office and write an ad describing

their ideal candidate. Ads should include the skills needed for the job.

As a follow-up activity, post these ads on the bulletin board, grouping them by elective office, and national, state, or local level of government. As students learn about different candidates, have them pick one of the ads to answer. Have students write a letter telling why they think the candidate they have selected would be right for the job.

Speaking Up and Speaking Out

Discuss with students the differences between facts and opinion. Explain to students that the editorial page is a good place to read people's opinions on issues that are important to voters. Editorial pages often express how a newspaper's editors or publisher feel about issues of national or local interest. Point out to the class the different types of features typically found on an editorial page: editorials by staff, syndicated columnists, local guest columnists, letters to the editor, political cartoons. As a class, name some of the key issues that concern people in your community now. Often these issues relate to schools, road construction, crime, housing, government spending, public services such as police or sanitation, and environmental problems. Working in groups, have students use the Activity Page 43, *Your Opinion Please*, to analyze the editorial page.

Making Your Voice Heard: Letters to the Editor

After reading and analyzing the editorial page, have students pick one of the letters to the editor and write a response to it in the second part of Activity Page 44. Prior to assigning this activity, post on the bulletin board copies of five or six letters that students might wish to respond to. Before having students work on their own, you may want to pick one letter and discuss with the class the elements that might go into their responses. In responding students might follow these guidelines:

1. State the problem as the writer has explained it.

2. Explain why you agree or disagree with the writer's description of the problem.

3. Explain why you agree or disagree with the writer's solution to the problem.

4. Describe how you would solve the problem.

The Kid Who Ran for President
by Dan Gutman
Scholastic, 1996

About the Book

In this satire of the political process, Judson Moon, a wisecracking twelve-year-old, decides to run for President. In the weeks that follow, Moon stumbles through all the steps in a national campaign. He selects his polar opposite for a running mate. June Syers is an elderly African-American woman confined to a wheelchair who hasn't voted in a presidential election since she voted for FDR. "Moon and June" get on the ballot in their home state, garner lots of publicity, collect millions in campaign contributions, and even help to pass an amendment to the Constitution that eliminates the age requirement for the presidency. In the end, despite a skeleton in his closet from the fourth grade, Judson wins the election. Fortunately, reality sets in and he resigns before even taking office, asking voters "Are you out of your minds?"

The Kid Who Ran for President is a presidential campaign turned upside down. Moon knows absolutely nothing about politics or the Constitution when his campaign starts, but he is a quick learner. Gutman's presentation of the media circus that surrounds a campaign is hilarious.

As You Read

Have students keep a list of the steps that Judson Moon and his wily campaign manager, Lane Brainard, follow to get Judson into the White House. Ask students to compare each step Judson takes on the path to the White House to the steps in an active presidential campaign. For example, Moon receives money, mostly from children, without working very hard for it. How much money do the current candidates have in their war chests? How do they collect it? Ask students:

❧ *How does Gutman poke fun at the political process?*
❧ *At several points, Moon tries to sabotage his own campaign. Why do his attempts fail?*

After You Read

It takes an amendment to the Constitution to allow Judson Moon to run for president, because the Constitution says a president must be at least 35 years old. What are the other requirements to be president? Read the Constitution or look in an encyclopedia to find out.

If you could interview the author of the book, Dan Gutman, what would you ask him? Write three questions that you would like to ask Mr. Gutman about his book, politics in general, or even the current election.

Extension
Write a new conclusion to *The Kid Who Ran for President* in which Judson Moon does not resign from office. Before you begin writing, look at some recent newspaper articles about the current president's activities. Think what Judson Moon might have done in similar circumstances. Then decide what kind of fun Judson would have as president, what sort of mistakes he might make, and whether he would be able to accomplish anything. Decide how Judson's presidency ends. Does he finish his term or is he forced to resign?

Analyzing Television Coverage of Elections

For many voters today, television is the major source of information about candidates for public office. Candidates come into our homes through our television sets in many different forms: commercials, newscasts, debates, talk shows, and panel discussion. Discuss the differences among these types of election television coverage.

- *Which are likely to be the most objective? the most biased?*
- *Which tell the viewer only what the candidate wants us to hear?*
- *Do some types of television coverage give a clearer idea than others of a candidate's views on issues?*

Creating a Media Log
Have each student pick a candidate who is likely to receive a lot of coverage on local and/or national news. Distribute copies of the media logs on Activity Page 45. Have students watch the nightly news for five days and fill in the log each time their candidate is mentioned. After students have completed their media logs, you might want to use these questions to generate discussion.

- *What can you learn about a candidate from watching television news? Can you learn about his or her views on issues? qualifications for the office? personal life?*

- *Can you learn enough from television news to make an informed decision about voting for that candidate?*
- *Did some candidates use the media more effectively than others? Give examples.*
- *What are some other ways to learn about local candidates? about the candidates for President?*

Comparing Network News

Divide students into several teams. Ask each group to watch the nightly news on one of the major networks for three days, using Activity Page 46 to record coverage of election news. One student in each group can be the timekeeper, keeping track of the amount of time the news show devotes to election news. Other group members can write two or three sentences describing the content of the reports. At the end of the three days, have groups prepare a group report based on their logs. Use them to compare and contrast nightly news coverage of the election on the different networks. Ask students:

- *Which network gave the most time to election news during this period?*
- *Did any give in-depth reports or analyses on candidate's views or experience?*

Be Ad Smart

If possible, videotape and bring to class four or five examples of political campaign advertising. Be prepared to show each ad several times. Show students examples of both positive and negative political advertisements. Explain to students that in a positive political ad the candidate, his or her party, and/or the issues he or she supports are shown in a favorable light. The ad stresses the candidate, his or her family attachments, career achievements, and stands on issues. A negative political ad portrays the opposing candidate in an unfavorable light. A goal of negative advertising is to make voters doubt the opposing candidate, his political party, or policies and the wisdom of his or her stands on issues. Point out to students any examples of negative campaigning in the ads. Then have each student pick one advertisement and analyze it, using the questions on the Activity Page 47, *Be Ad Smart.*

The Art of Propaganda

Candidates naturally want the strongest, most effective advertising they can buy. However, political advertisements often use propaganda, which is information that promotes a certain set of beliefs and opinions. In propaganda, opinions are often presented as facts. Usually propaganda is one-sided and does not tell the whole story. Listed below are some of the most common forms of propaganda.

- *Name Calling* Giving an idea or opponent a bad name.
- *Plain Folks* Showing viewers that the candidate is "one of us," just an ordinary person.
- *Card Stacking* Using facts and figures that favor one position while leaving out the facts and figures that support the other side.
- *Bandwagon* Convincing us to vote for a candidate because he or she is the most popular.

- *Testimonial* Having some well-known person voice their support for a candidate.
- *Empty Phrases* Using broad statements which mean little but which create positive feelings, such as: "I believe in freedom, peace, and the American way."

Have students view one of the video campaign advertisements introduced in the section *Be Ad Smart*. Using Activity Page 48, *You Can't Fool Me*, help students pick out examples of the different propaganda techniques listed above.

Ready, Camera, Action
Working in groups, have students use Activity Page 49 to create a story board for a 60-second television commercial for a well-known historical figure such as George Washington, Abraham Lincoln, or Thomas Jefferson. Each group will need multiple copies of the storyboard for this activity. Before beginning, have students identify the office the candidate is running for, the audience they would like to reach with their message, and what they want voters to know about their candidate. Encourage students to make up slogans for their candidate and include in their ads some of the candidate's views and qualifications. Using their storyboards as a guide, have students act out their commercials for the class. After each group has presented its ad to the class, students might use their Activity Sheet 47 *Be Ad Smart* to evaluate one another's ads.

The Incumbent Advantage
In most political races there is an *incumbent*, a person already holding a political office, and a *challenger*. Typically, the incumbent has a slight advantage over the challenger. Have students suggest reasons why this might be. During the campaign period, the President and other incumbents running for reelection make public appearances as part of their job. The activities of the President, members of Congress, governors, and other high officials often make the news, giving these candidates free air time on radio and television. Television viewers see the President, for example, in a positive light as he carries out the duties of his office—making announcements from the White House, giving federal grants to states, visiting disaster victims.

Students can see for themselves the incumbent advantage by tracking the appearances of an incumbent and challenger on nightly news for one week. Students can divide a sheet of paper in half lengthwise, label one side *incumbent* and the other *challenger* and make a mark each time the incumbent's name is mentioned and each time the challenger's name is mentioned. At the end of the week, have stu-

dents add up the marks in each column and compare results.

Politics in Your Mailbox

As the election heats up, voters often receive campaign literature in the mail. Direct mail, or mass mailings sent to selected voters asking for support, is a form of campaign advertising. This type of campaign advertising usually has two purposes: to ask for money for the candidate and to gain votes. Often these letters are written by professional fundraisers hired by the candidate. Members of different groups may receive different versions of the same letter. For example, a person running for the state legislature might send one letter to members of a teachers' organization and a different letter to members of a veterans' organization. Have each student bring in an example of direct-mail campaign literature. Have students analyze the letters by considering the following questions:

❧ *Who wrote the letter? What is this person's connection to the candidate? Underline two or three sentences that tell why this person is writing to you.*

❧ *What does the letter writer want you to do?*

❧ *Can you learn anything from this letter about the candidate's stands on campaign issues? about the candidate's qualifications for office?*

❧ *Does the campaign literature mention the candidate's opponent? If so, are any criticism or charges against the opponent backed up with facts?*

Making Graphs and Taking Polls

In these activities students make graphs using election data they create themselves and analyze election data provided for them. They also take their own polls and think critically about public opinion polls reported in the press.

Graph It

Have students nominate candidates for best book, best television show, best song, best movie, or best place to visit in the state. Try to pick a topic and candidates that are popular with a wide range of students. Select four nominees. Have students in the class vote by a show of hands. Tally results on the board and then break down the results in four ways:

1. Total votes for each candidate.

2. Number of girls voting for each candidate.

3. Number of boys voting for each candidate

4. Number of students who watch 6 or less hours of television and students who watch more than 6 hours of television each week voting for each candidate.

Write the results of the vote in each of these categories on a large sheet of poster board and post it on the bulletin board.

Working individually or in small groups, have students use Activity Page 50, *Graph It*, to make simple bar graphs of the information shown on the board. Depending on the ability level of students, each group can make one graph or all four graphs. After each graph is completed, have the group write a sentence describing what they have learned about voters from graphing the information in each way. Students may find that some graphs give them more useful information about voting patterns than others. Advanced students might want to also create circle graphs from the information and then compare the different ways the graphs present information.

DID YOU KNOW?
A 1998 Kids Voting Poll reported that close to 77 percent of students and 72 percent of adults cited television newscasts as their most important source for news about candidates and issues.

Using a Graph to Predict Voter Turnout

Students can use Activity Page 51, *Americans at the Polls*, to make a line graph of voter turnout in recent presidential elections. For statistics on more recent elections, students can consult a current almanac. When the graph is completed, have students look for any trends in voter turnout. From 1968-1988, voter turnout generally declined. In 1992, the percentage of Americans voting rose to its highest level since 1972. However in 1996, it dropped again to slightly less than in 1988.

Ask students whether they think the general trend toward low voter turnout is continuing or whether a new trend is beginning.

Polls and Pollsters

Explain to students that polls represent a "snapshot in time." Polls show how people feel about a topic at a certain time, but do not necessarily indicate how people will feel about this same subject a week or a month later.

Give students practice in polling by having them take a school-wide poll. As a class decide on a topic and a set of choices for the survey. At lower grades, students might choose favorite animals. (Which of these animals would you choose for school mascot? bear, leopard, cobra, alligator). For the upper grades, students might sample school opinion on local or national issues or issues that concern students at the school, such as the environment. (Which of these issues concerns you the most?) Or students can be polled on their choices for President. (If the election for President were held today, would you vote for [candidate A] or [candidate B]?) Ask students to poll 20 or 30 students at each grade level in the school. In recording responses, pollsters should be sure to record the gender and grade level of respondents. Some students can also be assigned to poll teachers. When the poll is completed, students can use Activity Page 50 to create a bar graph of their findings. Compare poll findings for the different groups polled: boys, girls, teachers, fifth graders, etc.

Analyzing a Poll

Bring to class a political poll or survey from a newspaper or newsmagazine. Also bring any articles that include conclusions that have been drawn from the poll results. As a class analyze the poll using these questions:

- *What questions were asked in the poll?*
- *Who was asked?*
- *How were the people who were polled chosen?*
- *How large a group was polled?*
- *Who sponsored the poll?*
- *When was the poll taken?*
- *Was the poll affected by a key event such as a military crisis, a natural disaster, or political scandal?*
- *Do you think answers to this poll might change if these same questions are asked in a week? in a month?*
- *Were any of the questions slanted or biased?*
- *Did any of the questions encourage the person polled to answer in a certain way?*
- *What conclusions did the pollster or reporter draw from the responses?*

DID YOU KNOW?

An exit poll is a special type of poll that pollsters take on election day while the polls are open. This is a poll taken of voters just after they have voted and are exiting the polling place. On election night, television commentators usually use these polls to make victory predictions before all the votes have been counted. Sometimes these predictions are wrong, as in the 1948 presidential election when some experts mistakenly predicted that Thomas Dewey would beat Harry Truman. In fact, Truman won with 51% of the vote.

Name _____

Election News Scavenger Hunt

Find eight of the items on the list in the newspaper you have been given, and check them off the list. Be sure to write down the page number on which you found each item.

Name of my newspaper _____

Date _____

Item	Page Number
1. Photo of a candidate ✔ _____	_____
2. Headline about a candidate or election _____	_____
3. Quotation from a candidate _____	_____
4. Article about a candidate running for national office _____	_____
5. Article about a candidate running for state office _____	_____
6. Article about a candidate running for local office _____	_____
7. Names of two elected offices (for example, mayor or governor)_____	_____
8. Name of the Democratic Party_____	_____
9. Name of the Republican Party _____	_____
10. Letter to the editor about an election_____	_____
11. Editorial about an election _____	_____
12. A cartoon about campaigns or elections _____	_____

Name _____

Your Opinion Please

1. Check any of the features listed below that you find on the editorial page you have been given.

___ letters to the editor   ___ editorials by members of the newspaper staff
___ political cartoons   ___ comic strips
___ local guest columnists   ___ political cartoons
___ syndicated columnists

Describe any other features on the page not listed above._____
_____

2. Describe one issue that concerns the editors of the newspaper you have been given._____
_____
_____

3. What does the editor who wrote the editorial think should be done about this issue?_____
_____
_____

4. Did you find any editorials or cartoons about local issues that directly affect or concern people in your community or state?
Give one example of a local issue_____
_____

Did you find any editorials or cartoons about national issues that affect people throughout the United States? _____

Give one example of a national issue _____
_____

5. List five words that the editorial writer uses that show that this is an opinion rather than fact.

     1. _____
     2. _____
     3. _____
     4. _____
     5. _____

Name _____

The Soundoff Sentinel
N E W S

1. Describe one issue that concerns someone who has written a letter to the editor. Attach a copy of this letter to this activity sheet. _____
_____
_____
_____
_____

2. Write your own letter in response to a letter to the editor that has appeared in the newspaper.

Dear _____ :
_____
_____
_____
_____
_____
_____
_____
_____
_____
_____
_____
_____
_____
_____

3. Choose an issue in your community or school about which you feel strongly, such as a recycling program, a new playground, or a new building or highway. Write a letter to the editor of your local newspaper or school newspaper expressing your opinion on this issue.

Name _____

Media Watch Log

Date	Summary of News Item	Helpful or Harmful to the Candidate?
_____	_____	Helpful _____ Harmful _____
_____	_____	Helpful _____ Harmful _____
_____	_____	Helpful _____ Harmful _____
_____	_____	Helpful _____ Harmful _____
_____	_____	Helpful _____ Harmful _____

Name _____

Television Election Log

Television Network _____
Time of Broadcast _____
Name of Show_____

Date	Summary of News Item	Length of Item in Minutes	Candidates' Views Yes No

Total Time _____ minutes

Name _____

Be Ad Smart

Use this page to study the secret meaning of a candidate's television advertisement and to find out the story behind the story. Write your answers on the back of this page.

Name of Candidate

_____

_____

Position he or she is running for _____

1. Does the candidate appear in the ad? If so, what is he or she doing?
2. Do any other people appear in the ad with the candidate? If so what is their part in the ad?
3. What did you learn about the candidate's stand on issues?
4. What did you learn about the candidate's qualifications for public office?
5. Did the candidate try to influence your opinion of his or her opponent? If so, in what way?
6. Were music or sound effects important to the overall impression of the ad?
7. Was the setting important to the overall impression of the ad?
8. Does the ad use any special slogans to get the candidate's message across?
9. What group of people did the makers of this ad want to appeal to? For example, was this ad aimed at all voters, younger voters, women, senior citizens?
10. What special images or props were used?
11. What impression did you have of the candidate from viewing this ad?
12. Do you think this is the impression the candidate wanted you to have? Explain

Name _____

You Can't Fool Me: The Art of Propaganda

Propaganda comes in many different flavors. Use this page to examine a campaign advertisement and to keep track of the different types of propaganda that the candidate uses.

Type of Propaganda	Example
Name Calling	
Plain Folks	
Card Stacking	
Bandwagon	
Testimonial	
Empty Phrases	

Name _____

Ready, Camera, Action

Script— Scene # _____

_____

_____

_____

_____

Visual — Scene # _____

Script— Scene # _____

_____

_____

_____

_____

Visual — Scene # _____

Script— Scene # _____

_____

_____

_____

_____

Visual — Scene # _____

Name _____

Graph It

Use the voting information your teacher has given you to complete these graphs.

BOYS AND GIRLS

30
25
20
15
10
5
0

1 #1_____ #2_____ #3_____
C A N D I D A T E S

BOYS

30
25
20
15
10
5
0

2 #1_____ #2_____ #3_____
C A N D I D A T E S

GIRLS

30
25
20
15
10
5
0

3 #1_____ #2_____ #3_____
C A N D I D A T E S

TV WATCHERS

30
25
20
15
10
5
0

More than 6 Hours of TV Less than 6 Hours of TV   More than 6 Hours of TV Less than 6 Hours of TV   More than 6 Hours of TV Less than 6 Hours of TV

4 #1_____ #2_____ #3_____
C A N D I D A T E S

1. What I have learned from Graph 1 ? _____
_____

2. What I have learned from Graph 2? _____
_____

3. What I have learned from Graph 3? _____
_____

4. What I have learned from Graph 4 ? _____
_____

50

Name _____

Americans at the Polls

Use the information below to complete this graph. You might also include data about more recent elections by researching in an almanac or encyclopedia. Draw points for each of the years and then connect the points to form a line graph.

Voter Turnout in U.S. Presidential Elections, 1968-2004

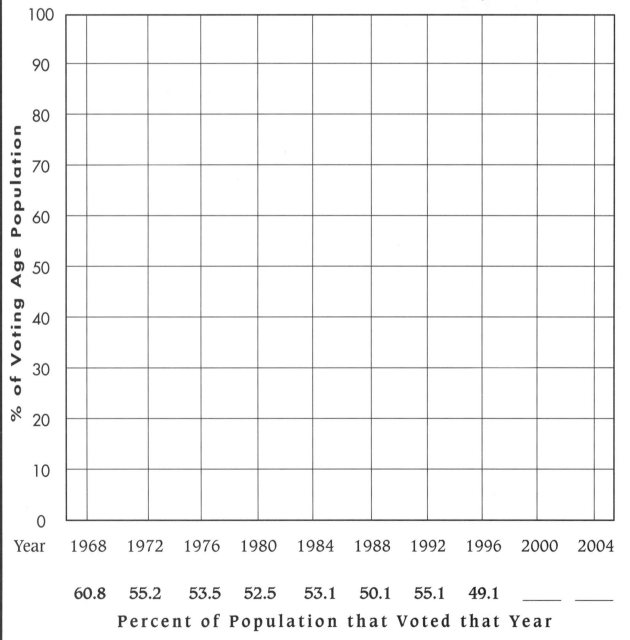

Year	1968	1972	1976	1980	1984	1988	1992	1996	2000	2004
	60.8	55.2	53.5	52.5	53.1	50.1	55.1	49.1	____	____

Percent of Population that Voted that Year

ELECTION FEVER

During an election year, political activity in the United States reaches a fever pitch. Much of the excitement revolves around the two main political parties, the Democratic Party and the Republican Party. Although independent candidates have long exerted some influence on American politics, we still basically have a two-party system. In the following activities, students will gain an understanding of the role that these parties play in campaigns and elections.

Election fever reaches its height right before the one day in November when everything is decided—Election Day. Students will learn about what happens on this important day and have a chance to simulate an election of their own.

Understanding Political Parties

Although you won't find political parties mentioned in the Constitution, they are very much a part of the American political system. In his Farewell Address to Congress, President George Washington warned against the harmful effects of political parties, believing they would do little more than divide the country. The first political parties were formed in the 1790s when Alexander Hamilton and Thomas Jefferson competed for President. Hamilton and his followers became known as the Federalists, while Jefferson's supporters became the Democratic-Republicans or Anti-Federalists. By 1809, the Federalist Party had lost many of its supporters, but the Democratic-Republicans remained strong. By the 1820s the Democratic-Republicans were known simply as Democrats. They have remained one of the two major par-

DID YOU KNOW?

Cartoonist Thomas Nast introduced the elephant as the Republican Party symbol in an 1874 cartoon in Harper's Weekly. Andrew Jackson first used the donkey as a Democratic Party symbol after his opponents called him a "jackass" in the 1828 election. Some years later, after Nast used the symbol of the donkey for the Democratic Party in a cartoon, it became widely associated with the Democratic Party.

ties to this day. In 1854 opponents of slavery formed the Republican Party. This party was created to oppose the expansion of slavery into the western territories of the United States. Today the Republican Party is the nation's other major political party.

The major political parties play many important roles. They recruit candidates to run for office and help them to get elected. Political parties also help to get out the vote at election time. Another important role of political parties is to bring important issues to the public's attention. Candidates and party officials discuss these issues in pamphlets, press conferences, speeches and television appearances, helping citizens form opinions about them.

Design a Party Symbol

Have students describe some of the symbols associated with different political parties and discuss the different ways these symbols are displayed (banners, buttons, bumper stickers, posters). Ask students:

❧ *Why are political symbols important to a political campaign?*
❧ *Are they as important today as they were in the years before television?*

Have students work in groups to create a symbol for a new political party. Before beginning, students might consider what the party stands for and how the symbol might reflect their views. Have students pick a name their party. Students might choose an animal, flower, abstract design, or set of initials as their symbol. Remind students that the symbol should be simple, eye-catching, and easy to remember. For a bulletin board display, students can make larger drawings of their symbols on circles of heavy poster paper or oak tag. Or you can collect and display the symbols as a political button collage.

It's Party Time

Every four years the Republican Party and the Democratic Party hold national conventions. The most important activity at this convention is to nominate candidates for President and Vice President. Delegates also adopt a national party platform and make rules for governing the party. The convention usually lasts four days and is held in the summer months, during July or August, before the fall election. Here is a brief overview of what happens each day:

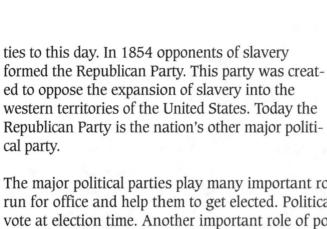

Day One: Delegates listen to the keynote address by a well-known member of the party. This speech is intended to whip up enthusiasm for the party. The speech sets the themes and the tone of the convention. Listeners also get a preview of the ideas and issues that the presidential candidate will stress in the election campaign ahead.

Day Two: Delegates discuss and accept the report of the Rules Committee which sets rules for the convention. The party platform, a statement of party principles and goals, is presented and approved by the delegates. The platform is prepared in advance by the Platform Committee which has worked for months before the convention to create a document that party members can agree upon.

Day Three: The party's candidate for President is nominated. Prominent or up-and-coming members of the party give the nominating speeches. These speeches are followed by seconding speeches. Then the clerk of the convention begins a roll call of the states. The chairperson of each state delegation announces into a microphone how many votes his or her state gives to each candidate. The roll call is in alphabetical order. Today the nominee is always chosen after one round of voting.

Day Four: The convention nominates the vice-presidential candidate. Since the election of Franklin Roosevelt, the vice-presidential candidate has been chosen by the presidential nominee of the party. The convention delegates always approve the vice-presidential nominee chosen. On the last night of the convention, the candidates for President and Vice President give their acceptance speeches. By tradition, the presidential nominee gives the final speech of the convention. This acceptance speech is considered a highlight of the convention.

Balancing the Ticket

When selecting a running mate, candidates for President often try to choose a vice-presidential candidate who will attract more and different voters. Often the presidential nominee looks for someone from a different part of the United States. They might also look for someone who is younger or older to appeal to different age groups or someone who is more or less liberal or conservative than they are. This process is called "balancing the ticket." By completing Activity Pages 63-64, students can decide for themselves how often geography was a factor in choosing a running mate for President in recent elections. (Students might work in groups to complete the pages. You might want to work together as a class to label all the states before proceeding on the main activity.)

And They're Off

After the national conventions, the race for the presidency switches into high gear. Candidates give speeches and more speeches, and travel across the country to rallies, dinners, and meetings. Candidates for other offices also work hard to promote their candidacies once the national convention is over. Candidates work to get their messages out to voters and spend more money on television, radio, and print advertising. The activities which follow give students a chance to explore the campaign process.

Day by Day

Contact the local campaign office of a candidate running for state or local office. Ask for a copy of the candidate's schedule for one week. Share this list with the class, looking at the types of events the candidate participated in and how these activities might have helped the candidate with his or her campaign. Ask students:

❥ *In what ways do you think the campaign schedule of an incumbent would be different from that of a challenger.*

Invite students to work with partners to track the campaign schedule of a candidate in a local, state, or national race for a week, using information from radio, television, and newspapers. Have them report their findings to the rest of the class.

On the Road with the Candidates

Post a large map of the United States on the bulletin board. Divide the class into campaign teams and assign each team one of the presidential candidates. Each team will follow their candidate on the campaign trail for a specified period of time. If the election has third party candidates, they should be included as well. Give each team different color push pins. Have students watch television and read newspapers and magazines to trace the movements of candidates on the map. Connect pins with colored yarn to show each candidate's movement during the campaign. Remind students of what they have learned about the Electoral College system. You may want to look at the Electoral College map on Activity Page 75. Have students list the top ten states in Electoral College votes and note the number of times their candidate has visited these states during the campaign. Ask students:

❥ *Which states were visited most?*
❥ *What might be reasons that these states were visited more than others?*

Step by Step to Good Speech Making

An important part of every candidate's campaign is making speeches. Many voters make their decisions about who they will vote for based on a candidate's speeches. Below are some steps to follow in delivering a convincing speech. You may want to share them with students and review them before the campaign simulation (see page 59), when students will have a chance to make campaign speeches of their own.

Planning Your Speech

1. Be prepared. You may be a little nervous, but that may a good thing Your nervousness may help you to put a little extra energy into your speech.

2. Consider your audience. What do you know about the group? What are their needs? Do they already agree with you? Or do you need to change their minds?

3. When you plan your speech, keep it simple. Use ordinary language and simple easy-to-follow sentences. Repeat your key points in different words.

4. Always begin with something to capture the attention of the audience—a joke, a story, an extraordinary statement, a challenge.

5. Stress what you want your audience to do—vote for you or vote for your candidate.

6. Timing is important. Don't speak too long; don't end too quickly.

7. End your speech with a summary of what you've said and a call to action—you want listeners to vote for you.

Practice, Practice, Practice

8. Practice saying your speech aloud. Ask your family and friends to listen to you and to offer suggestions. Videotape a rehearsal and then watch your performance.

9. Pay attention to your tone of voice and your gestures.

10. Do not read your speech. Use note cards or an outline. Speak directly to your audience as much as possible.

Delivering Your Speech

11. Look at your audience. Make eye contact.

12. Speak clearly. Don't speed up or go too fast.

13. Don't pace, scratch, or push your hair back. All gestures should have a purpose.

Analyzing Campaign Speeches

Videotape a televised speech by a candidate running for local, state, or national office. C-Span is a good place to find speeches for taping. Before showing the speech, distribute Activity Page 65, *Speech Scorecard*, and review the qualities students will be looking for as they review the speech. Activity Page 65 can also be used by students if they watch the televised presidential debates that occur close to Election Day.

Class President
by Johanna Hurwitz
Scholastic, 1991

About the Book

This book will help students to apply what they have learned about elections and campaigns to their own classroom and experiences. The novel's theme is leadership, specifically, what makes a good leader. At the beginning of the story, fifth-grader Julio equates leadership with popularity. He wants to help his friend win the election for class president. By the end of the story, with some help from his family, friends, and teacher, Julio learns that his own qualities of caring, courage, and fairness make him a leader—a class president.

As You Read

Ask students to keep a running list of words that describe Julio. As they learn new things about him and as Julio himself changes, students may add new words to their lists. For example, when the story begins, Julio lacks confidence. By the end of the book, Julio has learned to appreciate his strengths. To help students begin their lists, ask questions such as:

 ❧ *Why doesn't Julio tell anyone that he likes school lunches?*
 ❧ *Why does Julio pretend that he doesn't like school?*
 ❧ *Why hadn't Julio corrected his teachers when they mispronounced his name?*

After You Read

Ask students to think about the qualities that helped Julio win his class election. Ask students which of these qualities are important for a president or vice president and why they are important. For example, Julio shows courage by speaking to the principal about allowing soccer at recess. When does a United States president need to show courage? Then ask students to name qualities important for a President that were not mentioned or demonstrated in *Class President*.

Extension

Ask students to think about running for office. Ask them to make a list of their characteristics that would make them good candidates. Ask them to make another list of the characteristics that would hold them back in an election. Then ask students to write a speech nominating themselves for office. Tell them to stress their strengths.

Ask students to write a journal entry describing Julio's election from the point of view of Cricket Kaufman. Cricket thought she should be president, since she was a top student. What would she think about Arthur's song about Julio?

Classroom Campaigns and Elections

These activities offer a learning-through-doing experience. As students help plan an election campaign, they will have a chance to practice many of the skills they have learned in earlier activities, such as conducting a poll, creating a party symbol, and making and analyzing political ads and speeches. In the election simulation, students become aware of the consequences of the campaign as well as participating in the primary act citizenship—casting a ballot.

Race to Election Day

In this activity, students simulate the process of an actual campaign. At the lower grades, students might begin their simulation by voting for a book or author, television show, sport, pet, place to vacation, or food. You might want to use the candidates that students selected for their poll project in Section 2, page 41. Once the candidates have been picked, have students decide on criteria for judging the candidates. For example, if the class decides to vote on favorite desserts, students might assess their

choices in terms of taste, nutrition, calories, time to prepare, costs of preparation, visual appeal, and so on. Working in teams students can campaign for their favorite desserts, using posters, campaign buttons, or bumper stickers. They can

make short speeches in favor of their candidates. Several students can play the Election Board and register voters for the election following the directions outlined on page 20 of Section 1. On Election Day, set aside a corner of the room for voting with a large ballot box. Election Board members can enter the name of each voter in an election poll book on as each student comes to vote. Activity Page 66 contains a simple ballot that can be used for voting. After ballots have been counted and a winner declared, discuss with students how they made up their minds about which candidate to vote for.

➧ *What reasons did you have for your choices?*
➧ *Were you influenced by posters and other publicity? by campaign speeches?*
➧ *Did the candidate's ads say anything catchy you remembered?*
➧ *Was there any negative campaigning?*

Election Simulation

In this election simulation, students take on the roles of various participants in the in a presidential election campaign. The role cards on Activity Page 67, provide roles for the following:

a. Candidates: choose 2 students for these roles.

b. Campaign manager: you will need 2, one for each candidate.

c. Press secretary: you will need 2, one for each candidate.

d. Speech writer: depending on the class size, each campaign could have 2 or more.

e. Media consultant: You will need 2, one for each campaign.

f. Treasurer: you will need 2, one for each campaign.

g. Pollster: depending on class size, an "independent" polling organization used by both campaigns might consist of 3 or more pollsters.

h. Television reporter: depending on class size, 2 or more reporters.

i. Election Board member: you will need 3 Election Board members.

j. Voters: all remaining students.

Once role cards are distributed, give each candidate a certain amount of money (see Activity page 69 for currency). Each candidate can get $12,000 or to make the simulation more interesting and realistic, one candidate can get $10,000 and the other $14,000. Encourage Candidates to spend all their money. There is no advantage to having money

left over. You may want to point out to students that in a real campaign the financial resources of candidates are not equal. Have candidates give their money to their Treasurers. Give each Candidate, Treasurer, and the members of the Election Board a copy of Activity Page 70, The Rules for Spending Campaign Money and Price List for Campaign Activities. Post copies of these handouts on the classroom bulletin board.

After students have gotten into their assigned groups, distribute the appropriate Activity Card. There should be two groups made up of Candidates and Campaign Staff and one group each of Newspaper Reporters, Pollsters, Election Board members, Voters. After all groups have read over their Activity Cards, work with the class to determine the schedule of events that will make up the simulation. As the Activity Cards on pages 71-74 indicate, key events and activities can include television news broadcasts, press conferences, speeches by the candidates, registration, and voting. How much time students spend on these and other suggested activities will depend on how much time you have set aside for the simulation. There are several options and once the class has decided, you may want to make a time line to keep the simulation moving and on track.

Some classes may enjoy making up their own identities for candidates, but if students are having trouble getting started, you can also suggest identities for candidates. For example, one candidate might be a former governor from Texas

or from the students' home state. The other might be a former vice-president from Tennessee or a member of the Senate from New Jersey or from the students' home state. Or candidates can be modeled after individuals running for Congress or for local or statewide offices.

Be sure to review with Election Board members the registration process described on page 20 of this book. As candidates prepare their speeches, you might also have review pages 56-57, Step by Step to Good Speechmaking with them. You will need to work with the Television Reporters to decide when, where, and how they will hold their news broadcast and show political ads by candidates. If your class has access to a videocamera, ads and news shows can be taped and shown at a certain time each day of the simulation. Make sure that all students know that on Election Day everyone votes including Election Board members and candidates.

Election Night: Tracking the Election

Duplicate and distribute the student copies of the Election Map. Explain that on election day, students can use their maps to tally the electoral votes each candidate has won as this information is presented on television. Have students point out the sections of the country where election results would be reported first and ask them to explain why this is. As students are tracking election results, encourage them to look as well for "coattail's effects" and any sign of a "landslide" victory.

On the days following the election, have students conduct their own analysis of election results by using their colored-in maps. Draw a chart like the one below on the board. Volunteers can count the number of electoral votes each candidate received by region. Have them use newspapers to find out how many popular votes each candidate received in each region. Encourage them to use the chart to compare the electoral votes and popular votes for each region. Have them circle the winning party for each region. Were there any regions in which the popular vote was close? If so, students can consider how a slight change in the popular vote might have affected the final outcome of the election.

As a concluding activity, students working in groups can create five-minute television skits in which they act as media specialists or news anchors explaining the results of the election to their viewers. Their Election Maps can be used as visuals for their presentations.

	ELECTORAL VOTES	POPULAR VOTES
Northeast		
Republican Party		
Democratic Party		
Third Party		
Southeast		
Republican Party		
Democratic Party		
Third Party		
Midwest		
Republican Party		
Democratic Party		
Third Party		
Southwest		
Republican Party		
Democratic Party		
Third Party		
West		
Republican Party		
Democratic Party		
Third Party		

State and Local Link

To see how long the President's coattails were, students can compare election results in races for the House of Representatives and the Senate in their state with the vote for President in their state. Are newly elected members of Congress from the same political party as the President?

62

Balancing The Ticket

On the outline map, write the name of each candidate and the year of their election campaign in their home state. Draw a line connecting each candidate to his or her running mate. You might want to use different colors for different election years.

Year	Party	President	Vice President
1964	Dem	Lyndon Johnson (Texas)	Hubert Humphrey (Minnesota)
	Rep	Barry Goldwater (Arizona)	William E. Miller (New York)
1968	Dem	Hubert Humphrey (Minnesota)	Edmund Muskie (Maine)
	Rep	Richard Nixon (California)	Spiro Agnew (Maryland)
1972	Dem	George McGovern (South Dakota)	Sargent Shriver (Maryland)
	Rep	Richard Nixon (California)	Spiro Agnew (Maryland)
1976	Dem	Jimmy Carter (Georgia)	Walter Mondale (Minnesota)
	Rep	Gerald Ford (Michigan)	Robert Dole (Kansas)
1980	Dem	Jimmy Carter (Georgia)	Walter Mondale (Minnesota)
	Rep	Ronald Reagan (California)	George Bush (Texas)
1984	Dem	Walter Mondale (Minnesota)	Geraldine Ferraro (New York)
	Rep	Ronald Reagan (California)	George Bush (Texas)
1988	Dem	Michael Dukakis (Massachusetts)	Lloyd Bentsen (Texas)
	Rep	George Bush (Texas)	Dan Quayle (Indiana)
1992	Dem	Bill Clinton (Arkansas)	Al Gore (Tennessee)
	Rep	George Bush (Texas)	Dan Quayle (Indiana)
1996	Dem	Bill Clinton (Arkansas)	Al Gore (Tennessee)
	Rep	Robert Dole (Kansas)	Jack Kemp (New York)

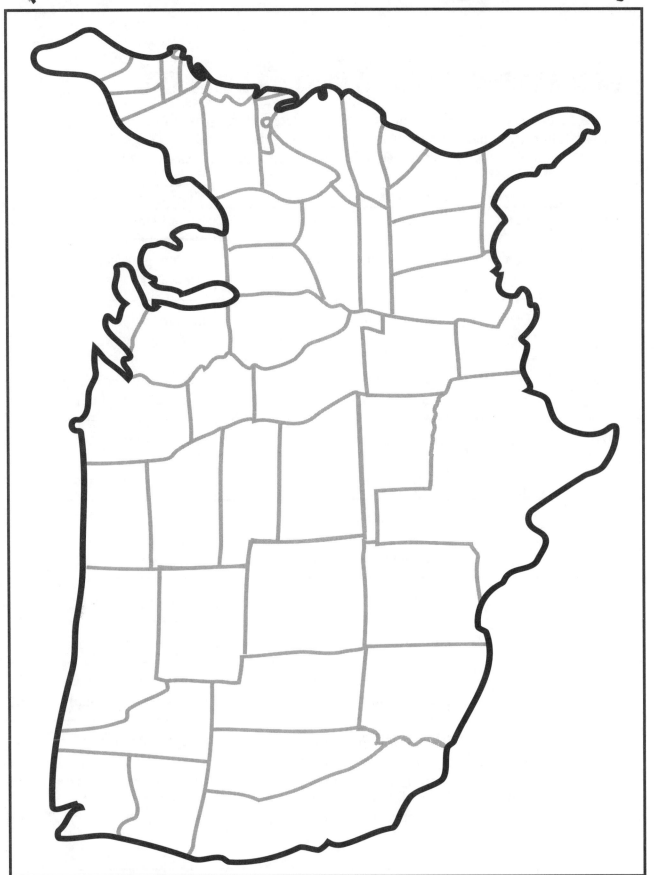

Name _____

Speech Scorecard

Use this scorecard to analyze a candidate's speech and to grade the various parts of the speech.

Speaker's Name _____
_____

Occasion for Speech
_____
_____

_____

Date _____

	Excellent	Good	Fair	Poor
Opening of speech				
Awareness of audience				
Organization of speech				
Choice of language				
Forcefulness				
Sincerity				
Eye contact				
Preparedness				
Gestures				
Length of speech				

I'd vote for the speaker   Yes   No

Official Ballot of _____

Office _____

☐	Candidate 1. _____
☐	Candidate 2. _____
☐	Candidate 3. _____
☐	Candidate 4. _____

Official Ballot of _____

Office _____

☐	Candidate 1. _____
☐	Candidate 2. _____
☐	Candidate 3. _____
☐	Candidate 4. _____

Election Simulation Role Cards #1

Candidate: You are running for the office of President of the United States. Your job is to campaign for office by making speeches, appearing in television campaign ads and at press conferences, and talking with voters about your goals and plans. You will need to work closely with your campaign manager to supervise the work of your campaign staff.

Campaign Manager: Your job is to supervise the work of your campaign staff. This group consists of a press secretary, speech writer, and media consultant. You can hire a polling organization to help you decide how well the campaign is going or to decide what issues voters care about. You will work closely with the candidate and the members of your staff to plan a campaign that makes your candidate and his or her ideas well known. You will also work closely with the Treasurer to decide how campaign advertising funds should be spent. Another part of your job is to recruit campaign workers from among voters to distribute fliers, put up posters, or take part in rallies.

Press Secretary: You will work with the campaign manager and media specialist to send out press releases about your candidate to the television reporters. You can hold a press conference and invite newspaper and television reporters to attend.

Speech Writer: Your job is to write election speeches for your candidate, telling why you think he or she should be elected. You can also create campaign posters, fliers, and brochures about your candidate and work with the media consultant on television ads.

Media Consultant: You are a media specialist. Your job is to plan your candidate's television commercials and any other advertising. You will be working hard to create a good image of your candidate. You will advise the candidate on how to dress for public appearances, what to say, and what campaign appearances to make. You can create political ads for your candidate and hire voters to act in your commercials. You will also work closely with the speech writers to prepare posters and any other campaign literature.

Election Simulation Role Cards #2

Treasurer: Your job is to work with the candidate and the campaign staff to decide how the campaign advertising money will be spent. Your job is to hold onto and keep track of the money given to your candidate, give it out when requested to do so by the candidate or campaign manager and let the candidate know often how much money has been spent. Your teacher will tell you how much money your campaign has to spend.

Pollsters: You belong to a company that conducts polls for political candidates. Your job is to find out what issues concern voters and report your findings to the candidates that hire you. You also take polls in which you question voters about their impressions of the candidate and find out how much support a candidate has. This information helps candidates plan their campaigns. Such information helps them make key decisions about how much money to spend on advertising and how this money can be spent wisely.

Television Reporter: Your job is to report on the campaign to the television audience on your daily news broadcast. You can interview the candidates at press conferences, analyze campaign ads, and report on speeches given by the candidates. You can also report the results of polls taken by pollsters.

Election Board Member: Your job is to supervise the election. You will need to find a polling place for students to vote on Election Day, make sure ballots are printed and direct the elections so that all students who have registered have a chance to vote. You will create a poll book, give out ballots, open and close the polls, and count the ballots, and announce the winner of the election.

Independent Voter: Your job is to listen to the campaign speeches of the candidates, participate in polls when asked, take part in campaign rallies or hand out leaflets for the candidate of your choice, register to vote, think carefully about which candidate would make the best President, and vote on election day.

Campaign Funds

Copy this page 8 times, cut out bills as indicated for a total of $24,000.
Use as currency for the *Election Simulation* on page 60.

CAMPAIGN $1,000. FUNDS $1,000.
ONE THOUSAND

CAMPAIGN $1,000. FUNDS $1,000.
ONE THOUSAND

CAMPAIGN $500. FUNDS $500.
FIVE HUNDRED

CAMPAIGN $500. FUNDS $500.
FIVE HUNDRED

The Rules for Spending Campaign Money

1. Campaign money can only be spent on these five items: television political ads, polls, campaign brochures, posters, and fliers.

2. Every time you make and show a political ad on television, you must pay the Election Board.

3. Every time you make and give out a new campaign brochure or flier, you must pay the Election Board.

4. Every time you put up a poster or have a new poll taken, you must pay the Election Board.

5. When you have spent your campaign money, you will not get anymore and you cannot borrow money from anyone else.

Price List for Campaign Activities

Show a Campaign Ad on television	$2500
Give out Campaign Brochure to voters	$1000
Give out fliers to voters	$500
Conduct a poll	$1500
Put up a poster	$500

Activity Card
Candidate and Campaign Staff

Candidate and Campaign Staff: (Campaign Manager, Press Secretary, Speech Writer, Press Secretary, Media Consultant, Treasurer)

a. Pick a party name and symbol.

b. Identify issues that the candidates and campaign staffs consider important and appealing to voters. These can be national issues, local issues, or schoolwide issues.

c. Decide on a budget for the campaign and make a list of ways for the candidate to get his or her ideas known to voters and the media.

d. Issue a press release to the media and/or fliers to voters announcing candidacy.

e. Contact polling organization or pollsters to conduct a poll to find out how voters feel about issues candidates have chosen to run on.

f. Hold a press conference or tape a political ad for television.

g. Make posters and fliers.

h. Recruit campaign workers to put up posters and give out campaign literature.

i. Hold a campaign rally.

j. Prepare a speech to be given before the election.

k. Hold a press conference to react to something the opposing candidate has said or done.

l. Challenge the opposing candidate to a debate.

m. Seek endorsements from members of the class and put them in campaign literature or post them on the bulletin board.

n. Hold another press conference or tape another political ad for television.

o. Try to get some free air time on television by staging a "photo opportunity" like a visit with voters.

p. Give an election speech at a rally or on television.

q. Election Day: Make sure campaign staff and campaign workers get out the vote.

Activity Card
Members of the Board of Elections

a. If voters have not registered, ask your teacher to make copies of the Voter Registration Form. Begin a voter registration drive. Put a sign on the bulletin board telling when the deadline for registering is. Try to get all class members to register. Explain that only people who have registered will be allowed to vote.

b. After the deadline for registration has passed, collect and alphabetize registration forms and create a Poll Book of all registered voters.

c. Find and set up a polling place for Election Day.

d. Fill in names of candidates and their political party on Official Ballot and make enough copies of the ballot for everyone in the class to vote.

e. Make a ballot box.

f. Post a copy of *The Rules for Spending Campaign Money* on the bulletin board and find out from the teacher how much money each candidate was given.

g. Decide how you will make sure that the rules for spending campaign money are being followed by all candidates.

h. Decide on penalties for spending money improperly and report these decisions to the television reporters, candidates, and campaign staff and voters.

i. Keep a list of how much money each candidate has spent and let candidates know when they have spent all of their money.

j. On Election Day open the polls and show the class that the ballot box is empty.

k. Before voters get their ballots, make sure their names are in the poll book. Be sure to mark off their names after giving them their ballots.

l. After everyone has voted announce th t the polls are closed and count the ballots.

m. Announce election results.

Activity Card
Pollsters

a. Make up a name for your polling organization.

b. Let candidates and news reporters know that you are a polling organization and will conduct polls for them. You may want to make an announcement on television or make a poster advertising your business.

c. When you are asked by the candidates to take a poll, make sure you understand what they want to find out from your survey.

d. Decide who you will survey for your poll and what questions you will ask.

e. Interview voters and analyze your results.

f. Make a graph showing your poll results.

g. Present your findings to the people who hired you to do the poll and share your poll results with the television reporters.

Activity Card
Television Reporters

a. Make up a call name and number for your television station like WVOTE or KNOW.

b. Decide which reporters will cover each campaign.

c. Begin to plan a 4- or 5-minute long Political News Update Show for your television station. The show can include campaign news, interviews with candidates, editorials by reporters or guest editorials, interviews with Election Board Members, interviews with pollsters, and reports on survey results.

d. Talk with your teacher to find out where and when your show will be and whether it will be live or taped and how often it will be on the air.

e. Attend all speeches, press conferences, rallies and other events given by candidates and bring a list of questions to ask candidates to all events.

f. Help the candidates and their campaign staffs decide when their political ads will appear on your tv station. Ads can be shown before, after, or during your news show.

g. Make public service announcements reminding people to register and vote.

h. On Election Day get the results of the election from the Election Board and report them on your news show.

Name _____

Election Night: Tracking the Election

Use the map below to track the election. Using a different color marker to represent the Democratic, Republican, or Third Party candidates, color in each state to show which party's candidate won the state's electoral votes. Be sure to complete the key.

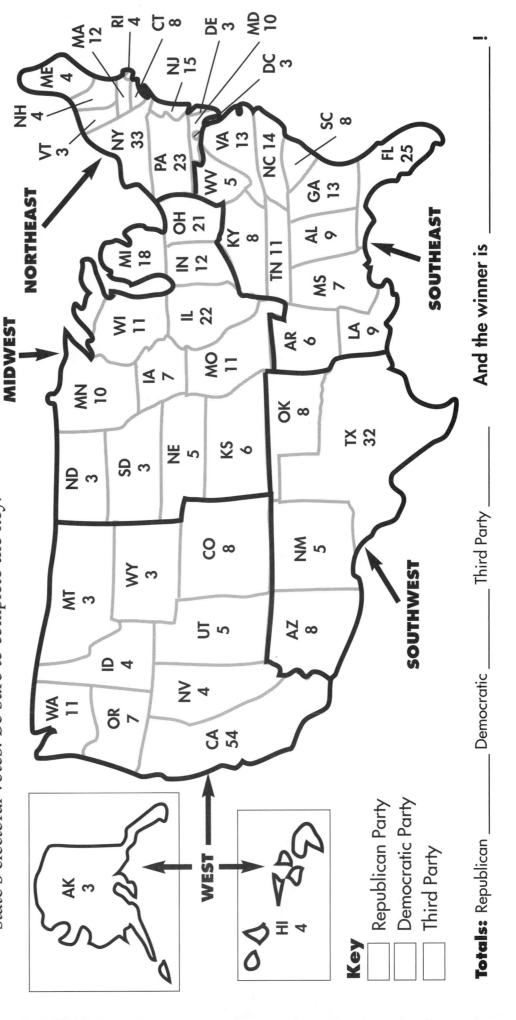

NORTHEAST

MIDWEST

SOUTHEAST

SOUTHWEST

WEST

State	Votes
ME	4
NH	4
VT	3
MA	12
RI	4
CT	8
NY	33
NJ	15
PA	23
DE	3
MD	10
DC	3
WV	5
VA	13
NC	14
SC	8
GA	13
FL	25
AL	9
MS	7
TN	11
KY	8
OH	21
IN	12
MI	18
WI	11
IL	22
MO	11
IA	7
MN	10
ND	3
SD	3
NE	5
KS	6
AR	6
LA	9
OK	8
TX	32
NM	5
AZ	8
CO	8
WY	3
MT	3
ID	4
UT	5
NV	4
CA	54
OR	7
WA	11
AK	3
HI	4

Key

☐ Republican Party
☐ Democratic Party
☐ Third Party

Totals: Republican _____ Democratic _____ Third Party _____

And the winner is _____ !

GLOSSARY

Ballot: a printed or electronic form used in voting.

Delegate: a person who is chosen to act for others at a meeting or convention

Democracy: a government of, by, and for the people, who have the right to choose their leaders

Direct Mail: mass mailings sent by candidates and political parties to selected voters asking for support and money

Electoral Votes: the votes cast by members of the electoral college. To win a presidential election, a candidate must win a majority of these votes.

Executive: the branch of government that enforces laws and is headed by the President

Exit Poll: a poll taken on election day as voters exit the polling place

Inauguration: the ceremony which includes the taking of an oath that takes place at the beginning of a President's term of office

Incumbent: a person already holding a political office

Judicial: the branch of government that interprets laws and includes the Supreme Court

Landslide: an overwhelming political victory

Legislative: the branch of government that makes the laws

National Convention: a meeting of members of a political party to nominate candidates to run for President, takes place in the summer months usually in July or August

Nominate: to propose a candidate for political office

Opinion Poll: a survey of people to find out what they think

Platform: a formal set of principles goals held by a political party

Political Party: a group of people who share similar ideas about how to govern the nation and work together to gain power by electing its members to public office

Polling Place: a place where votes are cast in an election

Presidential Election Day: the first Tuesday after the first Monday in November

Primary: an election between members of the same party who seek to be selected as their party's candidate

Propaganda: a form of communication that tries to spread and promote a certain set of beliefs

Registration: signing up to vote by filling in your name and other information about yourself on a special form

Sound Bite: a fragment of television videotape, usually nine or ten seconds in length

Third Party: a party organized as an alternative to the two major parties

Vote: a choice expressed by written ballot, voice, or a show of hands

Voter: a person who votes

RESOURCES

Books for Students

The President: America's Leader by Mary Oates Johnson (Steck-Vaughn Company, 1993)

The Vote: Making Your Voice Heard by Linda Scher (Steck-Vaughn Company, 1993)

Electing the President by Barbara Feinberg (Henry Holt & Company, 1995)

Presidential Elections by Miles Harvey (Children's Press, 1995)

Women's Voting Rights by Miles Harvey (Children's Press, 1996)

Elections in the United States by David Heath (Capstone Press, 1999)

The Presidential Elections by Christopher Henry (Franklin Watts, 1996)

The Voice of the People by Betsy and Guilio Maestro (Mulberry Books, 1998)

Organizations which provide voter education programs for students:

National Student/Parent Mock Election
225 West Oro Valley Drive
Tucson, AZ 85737
(520) 742-9943

Project Vote
Office of the Secretary of State
PO Box 12060
Capitol Station
Austin, TX 78711-2060
1-800-252-VOTE

League of Women Voters
1730 M Street, N.W.
Washington, DC 20036
(202) 429-1965

Project Vote Smart
129 NW Fourth Street, #204
Corvallis, OR 97330
1-800-622-7627

Web sites

Kids Voting
http://www.kidsvotingusa.org//
A teacher-developed site that includes grade-appropriate activities ready for downloading, on-line activities for kids, and links to other election-related sites.

CNN
http://cnn.com/ELECTION/2000
A great place to find up-to-the-minute coverage of the 2000 presidential race.

Federal Elections Commission
http://www.fec.gov/
Students may need your help to negotiate this site, but it's worth the effort. It includes loads of information on voter registration and turnout in recent elections.

Information Please
http://kids.infoplease.com
This easy-to-navigate site is an excellent place for students to research all aspects of our government.

World Media—Election Maps
http://www.worldmedia.fr/USelections
Here you can find colorful maps depicting the results of recent U.S. presidential elections.

Vote Smart
http://www.votesmart.org//
This is the web site of Project Vote Smart and it provides a wealth of facts on politicians including their biographies, issue positions, voting records, and campaign finances.

League of Women Voters
http://www.lwv.org/lwvus/
A good site to explore for information and tips on how to be a savvy voter. Includes a checklist that students can use to examine a candidate's stand on important issues.

RF

DC   E

m.

ce